LEARN BLUEJ PROGRAMMING

REFERENCE BOOK - PRACTICALS ONLY

AVINASH NANASAHEB PAGAR

I would like to dedicate this book to my all students.

Avinash Pagar

Contents

CHAPTER ONE

Program Introduction

Basic Programmes

1] Welcome to Blue J Programming.

2] Addition of two number's.

3] Average of two integers data type number's.

4] Perform arithmetic operation +, -, * and /.

5] Convert given temprature from Farenheit degree into Centigrade degree.

6] Accept distance between two cities in km and display into meter, feet, inches and centimeters.

7] Calculate area of Circle.

8] Calculate area of Square.

9] Calculate area of Rectangle.

10] Calculate area and volume of Sphere.

11] Calculate Roots of quadratic equation ax2+bx+c.

12] Calculate a Simple Interest.

13] Calculate the sum of first and last digits 4 digit no.

14] Swap value of A & B using temporary variable.

15] Swap value of A & B without temporary variable.

16] Calculate total no. Of Currency Notes of each denomination.

17] Calculate gross salary.

If Statement Programs

18] Check whether given no is even or odd.

18] Find maximum number between two number's.

20] Find maximum number between three number's.

21] Find minimum number between two number's.

22] Find minimum number between three number's.

23] Print Student Marksheet.

24] Check whether given year is leap or not.

25] Calculate profit & loss per item.

26] Find out triangle is valid or not.

27] Check type of character entered by user.

28] Perform multiplication operation without (*).

29] Check whether entered character is vowel or not.

While Loop Programs

30] Print infinite loop.

31] Calculate sum of digits of a given number.

32] Calculate product of digits of a given numbers.

33] Check whether the given no is magic or not .

34] Print reverse number of given number.

35] Check whether the given no is palindrome or not.

36] Print all the ASCII values and their equivalent characters.

'For Loop' Programs

37] Print the Series from 1 to 10.

38] Find X raise to Y.

39] Print the table of a given number.

40] Print the nth Fibbonacci series.

41] Find Maximum Number from 10 no's.

42] Find Minimum number from 10 no's.

43] Find Magic no from 1 to 1000 nos.

44] Find the palindrome nos. between 1 to 200.

45] Check whether given no is prime or not.

46] Print Prime number from 1 To 100.

47 Check whether given no is perfect or not.

48] Print perfect nos between 1 to 1000.

49] print all triplets(a,b,c) such that a2+b2=c2 where each a,b,c is between 1 and 50.

50] Find the factorial of given no.

51] Addition of N numbers.

52] Print all posssible combinations of 1,2,3 .

'Pattern' Programs

53] Print Star Triangle Pattern

```
*
* *
* * *
* * * *
* * * * *
```

54] Print Pattern.

```
1
2 2
3 3 3
4 4 4 4
5 5 5 5 5
```

55] Print Pattern.

```
1
1 2
1 2 3
1 2 3 4
1 2 3 4 5
```

56] Print Pattern.

```
1 1 1 1 1
2 2 2 2
3 3 3
4 4
5
```

57] Print Pattern.

```
5 4 3 2 1
5 4 3 2
```

```
5 4 3
5 4
5
```

58] Print Pattern.

```
1
2 3
4 5 6
7 8 9 10
11 12 13 14 15
```

59] Print Pattern.

```
1 2 3 4 5
6 7 8 9
10 11 12
13 14
15
```

60] Print Pattern.

```
* * * * *
* * * *
* * *
* *
*
```

61] Print Pattern.

```
A
B C
D E F
G H I J
K L M N O
```

62] Print Pattern.

```
A
B B
C C C
D D D D
E E E E E
```

63] Print Pattern.

A B C D E

F G H I

J K L

M N

O

64] Print Pattern.

A A A A A

B B B B

C C C

D D

E

65] Print Pattern.

A

A B

A B C

A B C D

A B C D E

66] Print Pattern.

A

B A

C B A

D C B A

E D C B A

67] Print Pattern.

E D C B A

D C B A

C B A

B A

A

68] Print Pattern.

1 2 3 4 5

1 2 3 4

```
1 2 3
1 2
1
```

69] Print Pattern.

```
1
1 2
1 2 3
1 2 3 4
1 2 3 4 5
1 2 3 4
1 2 3
1 2
1
```

70] Print Pattern.

```
1
2 2
3 3 3
4 4 4 4
5 5 5 5 5
4 4 4 4
3 3 3
2 2
1
```

71] Print Pattern.

```
1
1 1
1 1 1
1 1 1 1
1 1 1 1 1
```

Sum Of Series Programs

72] Calculate sum of series 1+2+3+4+_________+100.

73] Calculate sum of series 1!+2!+3!+....+10!.

74] Print serise 2 -4 6 -8 10 -12 14.....20.

75] Calculate sum of nth multiple of given no p.

Switch Statement

76] Check vowels using Switch Case Statement.

77] Convert numbers into words.

78] Print day name from week days by day number using switch case.

79] Print color name from colors list using switch case.

Array – One Dimensional

80] Find maximum no from given array.

81] Find smallest and largest no from 10 nos.

82] Search number from user input at runtime.

83] Calculate sum of element & average of one dimensional array.

84] Print one dimensional array.

85] Sort one dimentional array in an ascending order.

86] Sort one dimentional array in descending order.

87] Print array elements in reverse order.

88] Search element using linear search.

89] Search multiple occurrences of element using linear search.

90] Search element using binary Search.

91] Sorting method Bubble sort.

92] Sorting method Insertion sort.

93] Sorting method Selection sort.

94] Get number's find even, odd & sum of them.

95] Copy one array into another array in the revers order.

Matrix Programs - Two Dimension Array

96] Print the matrix (two dimensional array)

97] Search number from matrix.

98] Perform operation addition of two matrices.

99] Find minimum no from two dimentional array.

100] Find largest no from 3*3 matrix.

101] Sort two dimentional array.

102] Print even no from two dimentional array.

103] Print odd no from two dimentional array.

104] Print prime no from two dimentional array.

105] Calculate matrix multiplication.

106] Print Transpose Of matrix

107] Print the upper triangular matrix.

108] Calculate sum of upper triangular matrix.

109] Find minimum no from upper triangular matrix.

110] Find maximum no from upper triangular matrix.

111] Print lower triangular matrix.

112] Print minimum no from lower triagular matrix.

113] Print maximum no from lower triagular matrix.

114] Calculate sum of lower triagular matrix.

115] Print the identity matrix.

116] Calculate and print sum of row elements.

117] Calculate and print sum of column elements.

118] Calculate and print sum of row and column of matrix.

119] Find maximum number from row of matrix.

120] Find maximum number from column of matrix.

121] Find minimum number from row of matrix.

122] Find minimum number from column of matrix.

String Programs

123] Calculate string length using length() function.

124] Calculate string length without using length() function.

125] Compare Two Strings using compareTo.

126] Compare Two Strings using equals function.

127] Copy string using valueOf function.

128] Find character at given index location.

129] Find index of character.

130] Replace character in string.

131] Convert string into Uppercase.

132] Convert string into Lowecsae.

Function Programs

133] Addition of two nos. using function.

134] Area of circle using function.

135] Area of Square using function.

136] Area of Rectangle using function.

CHAPTER TWO

Basic Programs

1] Welcome to Blue J Programming.

```
public class Program1
{
public static void main()
{
System.out.println("Welcome To BlueJ");
System.out.println("Have a Good Day...");
}
}
```

Program Output

Welcome To BlueJ

Have a Good Day...

2] Addition of two numbers.

```
public class Program2
{
public static void main(int a,int b)
{
int sum;
System.out.println("First Number is = "+a);
System.out.println("Second Number is = "+b);
sum = a+b;
```

```java
System.out.println("Addition  Of  Two  Numbers  is
="+sum);
    }
}
```

Program Output

First Number is = 45

Second Number is = 65

Addition Of Two Numbers is =110

❧❧❧

3] Average of two integer's data type numbers.

```java
public class Program3
{
public static void main(int a,int b)
{
int avg;
System.out.println("First Number is = "+a);
System.out.println("Second Number is = "+b);
avg = (a+b)/2;
System.out.println("Average  Of  Two  Numbers  is
="+avg);
    }
}
```

Program Output

First Number is = 45

Second Number is = 65

Addition Of Two Numbers is =110

❧❧❧

4] Perform arithmetic operation +, -, * and /.

```java
public class Program4
{
public static void main(int a,int b)
```

```java
{
int sum,sub,prod,division;
System.out.println("First Number is = "+a);
System.out.println("Second Number is = "+b);
sum = a+b;
sub = a-b;
prod = a*b;
division = a/b;
System.out.println("Addition  Of  Two  Numbers  is  = "+sum);
System.out.println("Substraction Of Two Numbers is = "+sub);
System.out.println("Multiplication Of Two Numbers is = "+prod);
System.out.println("Division  Of  Two  Numbers  is  = "+division);
}
}
```

Program Output
First Number is = 72
Second Number is = 12
Average of Two Numbers is =42

❧❧❧

5] Convert given temperature from Fahrenheit degree into Centigrade degree.

```java
public class Program5
{
public static void main(int f)
{
double c;
System.out.println("Temperature in Fahrenheit = "+f);
c = 0.55*(f-32);
```

```
System.out.println("Temperature in Centigrade is = "+
c);
    }
}
```

Program Output

Temperature in Fahrenheit = 45
Temperature in Centigrade is = 7.15

❧❧❧

6] Accept distance between two cities in km and display into meter, feet, inches and centimeters.

```
public class Program6
{
public static void main(int d)
{
double meter,feet,inch,centi;
System.out.println("Entered distance in Km is = "+d);
meter = d * 1000;
feet = d * 1000 * 3.25;
inch = d * 1000 * 39;
centi = d * 1000 * 100;
System.out.println("Distance in Kilometers := "+d);
System.out.println("Distance in Meter := "+meter);
System.out.println("Distance in Feet := "+feet);
System.out.println("Distance in Inches := "+inch);
System.out.println("Distance    in    Centimeters    :=
"+centi);
    }
}
```

Program Output

Entered distance in Km is = 5
Distance in Kilometers: = 5
Distance in Meter: = 5000.0

Distance in Feet: = 16250.0
Distance in Inches: = 195000.0
Distance in Centimeters: = 500000.0

7] Calculate area of Circle.

```
public class Program7
{
public static void main(int r)
{
double pi=3.14;
double ac;
System.out.println("Radius of Circle Is :"+r);
ac = pi * r * r;
System.out.println("Area of circle is "+ac);
}
}
```

Program Output

Radius of Circle Is :5
Area of circle is 78.5

8] Calculate area of Square.

```
public class Program8
{
public static void main(float side)
{
float area;
System.out.println("Side of Ssquare Is := "+side);
area = side * side;
System.out.println("Area of Square is := "+area);
}
}
```

Program Output

Side of Square Is := 8.0

Area of Square is := 64.0

9] Calculate area of Rectangle.

```
public class Program9
{
public static void main(float l, float b)
{
float area;
System.out.println("Length is := "+l);
System.out.println("Breadth is := "+b);
area = l * b;
System.out.println("Area of Rectangle is := "+area);
}
}
```

Program Output

Length is := 7.0

Breadth is := 8.0

Area of Rectangle is := 56.0

10] Calculate area and volume of Sphere.

```
public class Program10
{
public static void main(float r)
{
double area, volume;
System.out.println("Radius of sphere is := ");
area = 4 * 3.14 * r * r * r;
volume = 1.33 *3.14 * r * r * r;
System.out.println("Area of sphere is := "+area);
```

```
System.out.println("Volume of sphere is := "+volume);
}
}
```

Program Output

Radius of sphere is := 3.0
Area of sphere is := 339.12
Volume of sphere is := 112.75740000000002

11] Calculate Roots of quadratic equation ax2+bx+c.

```
import java.io.*;
public class Program11
{
public static void main() throws IOException
{
Buffered  Reader  obj  =  new  BufferedReader(new
InputStreamReader(System.in));
    double a=0,b=0,c=0,x1=0,x2=0;
    System.out.println("Enter value Of a ");
    a = Double.parseDouble(obj.readLine());
    System.out.println("Enter value Of b ");
    b = Double.parseDouble(obj.readLine());
    System.out.println("Enter value Of c ");
    c = Double.parseDouble(obj.readLine());
    x1=((b * b)+ Math.sqrt(4 * a * c)) / (2 * a);
    x2=((b * b)- Math.sqrt(4 * a * c)) / (2 * a);
    System.out.println("The First Root is := "+x1);
    System.out.println("The Second Root is := "+x2);
}
}
```

Program Output

Enter value Of a
6

Enter value Of b
5
Enter value Of c
8
The First Root is := 3.2380338717125845
The Second Root is := 0.9286327949540819

12] Calculate a Simple Interest.

```java
import java.io.*;
public class Program12
{
public static void main() throws IOException
{
BufferedReader obj = new BufferedReader(new InputStreamReader(System.in));
double amount,rate,year,simpleint;
System.out.println("Enter principal amount :=");
amount = Double.parseDouble(obj.readLine());
System.out.println("Enter rate of interest :=");
rate = Double.parseDouble(obj.readLine());
System.out.println("Enter no. of years :=");
year = Double.parseDouble(obj.readLine());
simpleint = ( amount * year * rate )/100;
System.out.println("Simple Interest Is := "+simpleint);
}
}
```

Program Output

Enter principal amount :=
5000
Enter rate of interest :=
5
Enter no. of years :=

2
Simple Interest Is := 500.0

13] Calculate the sum of first and last digits 4-digit no.

```java
import java.util.*;
public class Program13
{
public static void main()
{
int num,sum=0,a;
Scanner scnObj = new Scanner(System.in);
System.out.println("Enter four digit no ");
num = scnObj.nextInt();
a = num/1000;
sum = sum + a;
a = num%10;
sum = sum+a;
System.out.println("Four-digit no is := "+num);
System.out.println("The sum of first and last digits 4 digit no := "+sum);
}
}
```

Program Output

Enter four digit no
1234
Four digit no is := 1234
The sum of first and last digits 4 digit no := 5

14] Swap value of A & B using temporary variable.

```java
import java.util.*;
public class Program14
```

```java
{
public static void main()
{
int a,b,temp;
Scanner scnObj = new Scanner(System.in);
System.out.println("Enter value of A := ");
a = scnObj.nextInt();
System.out.println("Enter value of B := ");
b = scnObj.nextInt();
temp = a;
a = b;
b = temp;
System.out.println("After Swapping");
System.out.println("Value of A "+a);
System.out.println("Value of B "+b);
}
}
```

Program Output

Enter value of A :=

8

Enter value of B :=

4

After Swapping

Value of A 4

Value of B 8

15] Swap value of A & B without temporary variable.

```java
import java.util.*;
public class Program15
{
public static void main()
{
```

```
int a,b;
Scanner scnObj = new Scanner(System.in);
System.out.println("Enter value of A := ");
a = scnObj.nextInt();
System.out.println("Enter value of B := ");
b = scnObj.nextInt();
a = a + b;
b = a - b;
a = a - b;
System.out.println("After Swapping");
System.out.println("Value of A "+a);
System.out.println("Value of B "+b);
}
}
```

Program Output

```
Enter value of A :=
56
Enter value of B :=
48
After Swapping
Value of A 48
Value of B 56
```

16] Calculate total no. of currency notes of each denomination.

```
import java.util.*;
public class Program16
{
public static void main()
{
int amt,hun,fifty,twenty,ten,five;
Scanner scnObj = new Scanner(System.in);
```

```java
System.out.println("Enter Amount := ");
amt = scnObj.nextInt();
hun=amt/100;
amt=amt%100;
fifty=amt/50;
amt=amt%50;
twenty=amt/20;
amt=amt%20;
ten=amt/10;
amt=amt%10;
five=amt/5;
amt=amt%5;
System.out.println("Hundred Rs. Notes :- "+hun);
System.out.println("Fifty Rs. Notes :- "+fifty);
System.out.println("Twenty Rs. Notes :- "+twenty);
System.out.println("Ten Rs. Notes :- "+ten);
System.out.println("Five Rs. Notes :- "+five);
}
}
```

Program Output

Enter Amount :=
485
Hundred Rs. Notes :- 4
Fifty Rs. Notes :- 1
Twenty Rs. Notes :- 1
Ten Rs. Notes :- 1
Five Rs. Notes :- 1

17] Calculate gross salary.

```java
import java.util.*;
public class Program17
{
```

```java
public static void main()
{
double basicpay,da,hra,grpay;
Scanner scnObj = new Scanner(System.in);
System.out.println("Enter Basic Salary := ");
basicpay = scnObj.nextDouble();
da=0.4 * basicpay;
hra=0.2 * basicpay;
grpay= basicpay + da + hra;
System.out.println("Basic Pay :- "+basicpay);
System.out.println("Dearness allowance "+da);
System.out.println("House rent allowance "+hra);
System.out.println("gross Pay "+grpay);
}
}
```

Program Output

```
Enter Basic Salary :=
20000
Basic Pay :- 20000.0
Dearness allowance 8000.0
House rent allowance 4000.0
gross Pay 32000.0
```

CHAPTER THREE

If Statement Programs

18] Check whether given no is even or odd.

```java
import java.util.*;
public class Program18
{
public static void main()
{
int num;
Scanner scnObj = new Scanner(System.in);
System.out.println("Enter value of A := ");
num = scnObj.nextInt();
if(num%2==0)
{
System.out.println("Number is Even ");
}
else
{
System.out.println("Number is Odd ");
}
}
}
```

Program Output

Enter value of A :=
18

Number is Even

19] Find maximum number between two numbers.

```java
import java.util.*;
public class Program19
{
public static void main()
{
int a,b;
Scanner scnObj = new Scanner(System.in);
System.out.println("Enter First No :- ");
a = scnObj.nextInt();
System.out.println("Enter Second No :- ");
b = scnObj.nextInt();
if (a > b)
{
System.out.println("Maximum Number is :- "+a);
}
else
{
System.out.println("Maximum Number is :- "+b);
}
}
}
```

Program Output

Enter First No :-

59

Enter Second No :-

78

Maximum Number is :- 78

20] Find maximum number between three numbers.

```java
import java.util.*;
public class Program20
{
public static void main()
{
int no1,no2,no3;
Scanner scnObj = new Scanner(System.in);
System.out.println("Enter First No :- ");
no1 = scnObj.nextInt();
System.out.println("Enter Second No :- ");
no2 = scnObj.nextInt();
System.out.println("Enter Third No :- ");
no3 = scnObj.nextInt();
if(no1 > no2 && no1 > no3)
{
System.out.println("Maximum number is :- "+no1);
}
else if(no2 > no1 && no2 > no3)
{
System.out.println("Maximum number is :- "+no2);
}
else
{
System.out.println("Maximum number is :- "+no3);
}
}
}
```

Program Output

Enter First No :-

46

Enter Second No :-

85

Enter Third No :-
62
Maximum number is :- 85

21] Find minimum number between two numbers.

```
import java.util.*;
public class Program21
{
public static void main()
{
int a,b;
Scanner scnObj = new Scanner(System.in);
System.out.println("Enter First No :- ");
a = scnObj.nextInt();
System.out.println("Enter Second No :- ");
b = scnObj.nextInt();
if (a < b)
{
System.out.println("Minimum Number is :- "+a);
}
else
{
System.out.println("Minimum Number is :- "+b);
}
}
}
```

Program Output
Enter First No :-
63
Enter Second No :-
47
Minimum Number is :- 47

22] Find minimum number between three numbers.

```java
import java.util.*;
public class Program22
{
public static void main()
{
int no1,no2,no3;
Scanner scnObj = new Scanner(System.in);
System.out.println("Enter First No :- ");
no1 = scnObj.nextInt();
System.out.println("Enter Second No :- ");
no2 = scnObj.nextInt();
System.out.println("Enter Third No :- ");
no3 = scnObj.nextInt();
if(no1 < no2 && no1 < no3)
{
System.out.println("Minimum number is :- "+no1);
}
else if(no2 < no1 && no2 < no3)
{
System.out.println("Minimum number is :- "+no2);
}
else
{
System.out.println("Minimum number is :- "+no3);
}
}
}
```

Program Output

Enter First No :-
74

```
Enter Second No :-
87
Enter Third No :-
32
Minimum number is :- 32
```

23] Print Student Marksheet.

```java
import java.util.*;
public class Program23
{
public static void main()
{
int m1,m2,m3,m4,m5,m6,total;
float per;
Scanner scnObj = new Scanner(System.in);
System.out.println("Enter Marks Of Maths :- ");
m1 = scnObj.nextInt();
System.out.println("Enter Marks Of English :- ");
m2 = scnObj.nextInt();
System.out.println("Enter Marks Of Science :- ");
m3 = scnObj.nextInt();
System.out.println("Enter Marks Of Computer :- ");
m4 = scnObj.nextInt();
System.out.println("Enter Marks Of History :- ");
m5 = scnObj.nextInt();
System.out.println("Enter Marks Of Hindi :- ");
m6 = scnObj.nextInt();
total = m1+m2+m3+m4+m5+m6;
per = (total) / 6;
System.out.println("Total is :- "+total);
System.out.println("Percentage is :- "+per);
if(per>75)
```

```java
System.out.println("Grade:Distinction");
else if(per<75 && per>=60)
System.out.println("Grade:First Class");
else if(per<60 && per>=50)
System.out.println("Grade:Second Class");
else if(per<50 && per>=35)
System.out.println("Grade:Third Division");
else
System.out.println("Grade:Fail");
}
}
```

Program Output

Enter Marks Of Maths :-
96
Enter Marks Of English :-
94
Enter Marks Of Science :-
90
Enter Marks Of Computer :-
92
Enter Marks Of History :-
90
Enter Marks Of Hindi :-
89
Total is :- 551
Percentage is :- 91.0
Grade:Distinction

24] Check whether given year is leap or not.

```java
import java.util.*;
public class Program24
{
```

```java
public static void main()
{
int year;
Scanner scnObj = new Scanner(System.in);
System.out.println("Enter Year :- ");
year = scnObj.nextInt();
if ( year%400 == 0)
{
System.out.println("Is a Leap Year");
}
else if ( year%100 == 0)
{
System.out.println("Is not a Leap Year");
}
else if ( year%4 == 0)
{
System.out.println("Is a Leap Year");
}
else
{
System.out.println("Is not a Leap Year");
}
}
}
```

Program Output
Enter Year :-
2016
Is a Leap Year

25] Calculate profit & loss per item.

```java
import java.util.*;
public class Program25
```

```java
{
public static void main()
{
float purpri,sellpri,profit,loss;
Scanner scnObj = new Scanner(System.in);
System.out.println("Enter cost price");
purpri = scnObj.nextInt();
System.out.println("Enter Selling price");
sellpri = scnObj.nextInt();
profit = sellpri - purpri;
loss = purpri - sellpri;
if(profit > 0)
{
System.out.println("Seller has made Profit of "+profit);
}
if(loss > 0)
{
System.out.println("Seller is in loss by :- "+loss);
}
if(profit == 0)
{
System.out.println("No Profit No Loss");
}
}
}
```

Program Output

Enter cost price

256

Enter Selling price

325

Seller has made Profit of 69.0

26] Find out triangle is valid or not.

```java
import java.util.*;
public class Program26
{
public static void main()
{
double first,second,third;
Scanner scnObj = new Scanner(System.in);
System.out.println("Enter first angle of triangle");
first = scnObj.nextInt();
System.out.println("Enter second angle of triangle");
second = scnObj.nextInt();
System.out.println("Enter third angle of triangle");
third = scnObj.nextInt();
if(first + second +third == 180)
System.out.println("Triangle is valid.");
else
System.out.println("Triangle is Not valid.");
}
}
```

Program Output

```
Enter first angle of triangle
45
Enter second angle of triangle
90
Enter third angle of triangle
45
Triangle is valid.
```

27] Check type of character entered by user.

```java
import java.util.*;
public class Program27
```

```
{
public static void main()
{
char ch;
Scanner scnObj = new Scanner(System.in);
System.out.println("Enter character :- ");
ch = scnObj.next().charAt(0);
if(ch>=65 && ch<=90)
System.out.println("The  character  is  an  uppercase
letter.");
if(ch>=97 && ch<=122)
System.out.println("The character is lowercase letter.");
if(ch>=48 && ch<=57)
System.out.println("The character is digit.");
if((ch>=0 && ch<48)||(ch>57 && ch<65)||(ch>90 &&
ch<97) || ch>122)
System.out.println("The character is special symbol.");
}
}
```

Program Output

```
Enter character :-
#
The character is special symbol.
```

❧❧❧

28] Perform multiplication operation without (*).

```
import java.util.*;
public class Program28
{
public static void main()
{
int i,a,b,prod=0;
Scanner scnObj = new Scanner(System.in);
```

```
System.out.println("Enter first number :-");
a = scnObj.nextInt();
System.out.println("Enter second number :-");
b = scnObj.nextInt();
for (i=1;i<=b;i++)
{
prod = prod + a;
}
System.out.println("Multiplication of two numbers is :-
"+prod);
}
}
```

Program Output

Enter first number :-

23

Enter second number :-

9

Multiplication of two numbers is :- 207

29] Check whether entered character is vowel or not.

```
import java.util.*;
public class Program29
{
public static void main()
{
char ch;
Scanner scnObj = new Scanner(System.in);
System.out.println("Enter character :- ");
ch = scnObj.next().charAt(0);
if ( ch == 'a' || ch == 'A' || ch == 'e' || ch == 'E' || ch == 'i'
|| ch == 'I' || ch =='o' || ch=='O' || ch == 'u' || ch == 'U')
System.out.println("The character is Vowel.");
```

```
else
System.out.println("The character is Not Vowel.");
}
}
```

Program Output

Enter character :-

A

The character is Vowel.

CHAPTER FOUR

While Loop Programs

30] Print infinite loop.

```java
import java.util.*;
public class Program30
{
public static void main()
{
int i=1;
while(i!=0)
{
System.out.println("Value of I is :- "+i);
i++;
}
}
}
```

31] Calculate sum of digits of a given number.

```java
import java.util.*;
public class Program31
{
public static void main()
{
int n,r,sum=0;
```

```java
Scanner scnObj = new Scanner(System.in);
System.out.println("Enter number :- ");
n = scnObj.nextInt();
while(n>0)
{
r = n%10;
sum = sum+r;
n=n/10;
}
System.out.println("Sum of Digits is :-"+sum);
}
}
```

Program Output

```
Enter number :-
4567
Sum Of Digits is :-22
```

❧❧❧

32] Calculate product of digits of a given numbers.

```java
import java.util.*;
public class Program32
{
public static void main()
{
int n,r,product=1;
Scanner scnObj = new Scanner(System.in);
System.out.println("Enter number :- ");
n = scnObj.nextInt();
while(n>0)
{
r = n%10;
product = product*r;
n=n/10;
```

```
}
System.out.println("Sum Of Digits is :-"+product);
}
}
```

Program Output

```
Enter number :-
2345
Sum Of Digits is :-120
```

33] Check whether the given no is magic or not.

```java
import java.util.*;
public class Program33
{
public static void main()
{
int n,r,sum=0,no;
Scanner scnObj = new Scanner(System.in);
System.out.println("Enter number :- ");
n = scnObj.nextInt();
no = n;
while(n>0)
{
r = n%10;
sum = sum+r*r*r;
n=n/10;
}
if (sum == no)
System.out.println("Number is Magic.");
else
System.out.println("Number is not Magic.");
}
}
```

Program Output

Enter number :-

370

Number is Magic.

34] Print reverse number of given number.

```java
import java.util.*;
public class Program34
{
public static void main()
{
int n,r,rev=0;
Scanner scnObj = new Scanner(System.in);
System.out.println("Enter number :- ");
n = scnObj.nextInt();
while(n>0)
{
r = n % 10;
rev = rev * 10 +r;
n = n/10;
}
System.out.println("Reverse No Is :- "+rev);
}
}
```

Program Output

Enter number :-

4567

Reverse No Is :- 7654

35] Check whether the given no is palindrome or not.

```java
import java.util.*;
```

```java
public class Program35
{
public static void main()
{
int n,no,r,rev=0;
Scanner scnObj = new Scanner(System.in);
System.out.println("Enter number :- ");
n = scnObj.nextInt();
no = n;
while(n>0)
{
r = n % 10;
rev = rev * 10 +r;
n = n/10;
}
if(rev == no)
System.out.println("No is Palindrome");
else
System.out.println("No is not Palindrome");
}
}
```

Program Output

Enter number :-
1234
No is not Palindrome

36] Display all the ASCII values and their equivalent characters.

```java
import java.util.*;
public class Program36
{
public static void main()
```

```java
{
int j=0;
while(j<=255)
{
System.out.println("ASCII Value of "+(char)j+" is "+j);
j++;
}
}
}
```

CHAPTER FIVE

For Loop Programs

37] Program to print the Series from 1 to 10.

```
import java.util.*;
public class Program37
{
public static void main()
{
int i;
System.out.println("The Series is");
for(i=1;i<=10;i++)
{
System.out.println(i);
}
}
}
```

Program Output

```
The Series is
1
2
3
4
5
6
7
```

8

9

10

❧❧❧

38] Find X raise to Y.

```
import java.util.*;
public class Program38
{
public static void main()
{
int a,n,i,prod=1;
Scanner scnObj = new Scanner(System.in);
System.out.println("Enter value of Base");
a = scnObj.nextInt();
System.out.println("Enter value of power");
n = scnObj.nextInt();
for(i=1;i<=n;i++)
{
prod=prod*a;
}
System.out.println(a+" Raised to "+n+" is "+prod);
}
}
```

Program Output

Enter value of Base

4

Enter value of power

3

4 Raised to 3 is 64

❧❧❧

39] Print the table of a given number.

```java
import java.util.*;
public class Program39
{
public static void main()
{
int no,i,table=0;
Scanner scnObj = new Scanner(System.in);
System.out.println("Enter number");
no = scnObj.nextInt();
System.out.println("The Table Of "+no);
for(i=1;i<=10;i++)
{
table=no*i;
System.out.println(table);
}
}
}
```

Program Output

```
Enter number
27
The Table Of 27
27
54
81
108
135
162
189
216
243
270
```

40] Print the nth Fibbonacci series.

```java
import java.util.*;
public class Program40
{
public static void main()
{
int n,f=0,f1=1,f2=1,i;
Scanner scnObj = new Scanner(System.in);
System.out.println("Enter order of series");
n = scnObj.nextInt();
System.out.println("Fibbonacci series.");
System.out.println(f1);
System.out.println(f2);
for(i=3;i<n;i++)
{
f=f1+f2;
System.out.println(f);
f1=f2;
f2=f;
}
}
}
```

Program Output

Enter order of series

10

Fibonacci series.

1

1

2

3

5

8

13

21
34

41] Find Maximum Number from 10 nos.

```
import java.util.*;
public class Program41
{
public static void main()
{
int no,i,max=0;
Scanner scnObj = new Scanner(System.in);
System.out.println("Enter 10 Numbers ");
for(i=0;i<10;i++)
{
no = scnObj.nextInt();
if(no>max)
max=no;
}
System.out.println("Maximum between 10 numbers is :-
"+max);
}
}
```

Program Output

Enter 10 Numbers
56
98
14
23
36
75
48
93

14
51
Maximum between 10 numbers is :- 98

42] Find Minimum number from 10 nos.

```java
import java.util.*;
public class Program42
{
public static void main()
{
int no,i;
int min= Integer.MAX_VALUE;
Scanner scnObj = new Scanner(System.in);
System.out.println("Enter 10 Numbers ");
for(i=0;i<10;i++)
{
no = scnObj.nextInt();
if(no<min)
min=no;
}
System.out.println("Minimum between 10 numbers is :-"+min);
}
}
```

Program Output

Enter 10 Numbers
45
32
56
89
74
58

96
49
74
56
Minimum between 10 numbers is :- 32

43] Find Magic no from 1 to 1000 nos.

```java
import java.util.*;
public class Program43
{
public static void main()
{
int n,no,r,sum=0;
System.out.println("The  Magic  nos.  between  1  to
1000.");
for(n=1;n<=1000;n++)
{
no = n;
while(no>0)
{
r = no%10;
sum = sum+r*r*r;
no=no/10;
}
if (sum == n)
System.out.println(n);
sum=0;
}
}
}
```

Program Output

The Magic nos. between 1 to 1000.

```
1
153
370
371
407
```

❧❧❧

44] Find the palindrome numbers between 1 to 200 numbers.

```
import java.util.*;
public class Program44
{
public static void main()
{
int n,no,r,rev=0;
System.out.println("Palindrome nos. between 1 To 200.");
for(n=1;n<=200;n++)
{
no = n;
while(no>0)
{
r = no % 10;
rev = rev * 10 +r;
no = no/10;
}
if(rev == n)
System.out.println(n);
rev=0;
}
}
}
```

Program Output

Palindrome nos. between 1 To 200.

1
2
3
4
5
6
7
8
9
11
22
33
44
55
66
77
88
99
101
111
121
131
141
151
161
171
181
191

45] Check whether given no is Prime or not.

```
import java.util.*;
```

```java
public class Program45
{
public static void main()
{
int n,i,pr=1;
Scanner scnObj = new Scanner(System.in);
System.out.println("Enter number :- ");
n = scnObj.nextInt();
for(i=2;i<n;i++)
{
if(n%i==0)
{
pr=0;
break;
}
}
if(pr==1)
System.out.println(n+" is Prime no.");
else
System.out.println(n+" is not Prime no.");
}
}
```

Program Output

Enter number :-
7
7 is Prime no.

***

46] Print Prime number from 1 to 100.

```java
public class Program46
{
public static void main()
{
```

```
int n,j,k,fact=0;
for(j=0;j<100;j++)
{
fact=0;
for(k=1;k<=j;k++)
{
if(j%k==0)
fact++;
}
if(fact==2)
System.out.println(j);
}
}
}
```

Program Output

```
2
3
5
7
11
13
17
19
23
29
31
37
41
43
47
53
59
61
```

67
71
73
79
83
89
97

47 Check whether given no is perfect or not.

```java
import java.util.*;
public class Program47
{
public static void main()
{
int n,no,i,fact=0;
Scanner scnObj = new Scanner(System.in);
System.out.println("Enter number :- ");
n = scnObj.nextInt();
no=n;
for(i=1;i<=n-1;i++)
{
if(n%i==0)
fact = fact+i;
}
if(fact==no)
System.out.println(n+" is Perfect no.");
else
System.out.println(n+" is not Perfect no.");
}
}
```

Program Output

Enter number :-

6

6 is Perfect no.

48] Print perfect nos between 1 to 1000 numbers.

```
public class Program48
{
public static void main()
{
int no,n,fact=0,i,j;
System.out.println("Perfect Nos.Between 1 To 1000.");
for(j=1;j<=1000;j++)
{
fact=0;
no=j;
for(i=1;i<=(j-1);i++)
{
if(j%i==0)
fact = fact+i;
}
if(fact==j)
System.out.println(no);
}
}
}
```

Program Output

Perfect Nos.Between 1 To 1000.

6

28

496

49] print all triplets(a,b,c) such that a2+b2=c2 where each a,b,c is between 1 and 50.

```java
public class Program49
{
public static void main()
{
int i=1,j,k,a,b,c;
for(i=1;i<=50;i++)
{
for(j=1;j<=50;j++)
{
for(k=1;k<=50;k++)
{
a = i*i;
b = j*j;
c = k*k;
if(c==(a+b))
System.out.println("a = "+i+" b = "+j+" c = "+k);
}
}
}
}
}
```

50] Find the factorial of given no.

```java
import java.util.*;
public class Program50
{
public static void main()
{
int n,i,fact=1;
Scanner scnObj = new Scanner(System.in);
```

```java
System.out.println("Enter number ");
n = scnObj.nextInt();
for(i=1;i<=n;i++)
{
fact=fact*i;
}
System.out.println("Factoirial of "+n+" is "+fact);
}
}
```

Program Output

```
Enter number
5
Factorial of 5 is 120
```

51] Addition of N numbers.

```java
import java.util.*;
public class Program51
{
public static void main()
{
int n, sum = 0, c, var;
Scanner scnObj = new Scanner(System.in);
System.out.println("Enter nos you want to add :-");
n = scnObj.nextInt();
System.out.println("Enter "+n+" nos");
for ( c = 1 ; c <= n ; c++ )
{
var = scnObj.nextInt();
sum = sum + var;
}
System.out.println("Sum of entered numbers "+sum);
}
```

```
}
```

Program Output

```
Enter nos you want to add :-
4
Enter 4 nos
55
110
65
75
Sum of entered numbers 305
```

52] Print all possible combinations of 1,2,3 numbers.

```
public class Program52
{
public static void main()
{
int p=1,q=1,r=1;
for(p=1;p<=3;p++)
{
for(q=1;q<=3;q++)
{
for(r=1;r<=3;r++)
{
System.out.println(p+""+q+""+r);
}
}
}
}
}
```

CHAPTER SIX

Pattern Programs

53] Print Star Triangle Pattern

```
*
* *
* * *
* * * *
* * * * *
public class Program53
{
public static void main()
{
int i,j;
for(i=1;i<=5;i++)
{
for(j=1;j<=i;j++)
{
System.out.print(" * ");
}
System.out.println();
}
}
}
```

Program Output

```
*
```

```
* *
* * *
* * * *
* * * * *
```

54] Print Numbers Pattern.

```
1
2 2
3 3 3
4 4 4 4
5 5 5 5 5
public class Program54
{
public static void main()
{
int i,j;
for(i=1;i<=5;i++)
{
for(j=1;j<=i;j++)
{
System.out.print(" "+i);
}
System.out.println();
}
}
}
```

Program Output

```
1
2 2
3 3 3
4 4 4 4
5 5 5 5 5
```

55] Print Number Pattern.

```
1
1 2
1 2 3
1 2 3 4
1 2 3 4 5
public class Program55
{
public static void main()
{
int i,j;
for(i=1;i<=5;i++)
{
for(j=1;j<=i;j++)
{
System.out.print(" "+j);
}
System.out.println();
}
}
}
```

Program Output

```
1
1 2
1 2 3
1 2 3 4
1 2 3 4 5
```

56] Print Number Pattern.

```
1 1 1 1 1
```

```
2 2 2 2
3 3 3
4 4
5
public class Program56
{
public static void main()
{
int i,j;
for(i=1;i<=5;i++)
{
for(j=5;j>=i;j--)
{
System.out.print(" "+i);
}
System.out.println();
}
}
}
```

Program Output

```
1 1 1 1 1
2 2 2 2
3 3 3
4 4
5
```

57] Print Number Pattern.

```
5 4 3 2 1
5 4 3 2
5 4 3
5 4
5
```

```java
public class Program57
{
public static void main()
{
int i,j;
for(i=1;i<=5;i++)
{
for(j=5;j>=i;j--)
{
System.out.print(" "+j);
}
System.out.println();
}
}
}
```

Program Output

5 4 3 2 1
5 4 3 2
5 4 3
5 4
5

58] Print Number Pattern.

1
2 3
4 5 6
7 8 9 10
11 12 13 14 15

```java
public class Program58
{
public static void main()
{
```

```
int i,j,a=1;
for(i=1;i<=5;i++)
{
for(j=1;j<=i;j++)
{
System.out.print(" "+a);
a = a+1;
}
System.out.println();
}
}
}
```

Program Output

```
1
2 3
4 5 6
7 8 9 10
11 12 13 14 15
```

59] Print Number Pattern.

```
1 2 3 4 5
6 7 8 9
10 11 12
13 14
15
public class Program59
{
public static void main()
{
int i,j,a=1;
for(i=1;i<=5;i++)
{
```

```java
for(j=5;j>=i;j--)
{
System.out.print(" "+a);
a = a+1;
}
System.out.println();
}
}
}
```

Program Output

```
1
2 3
4 5 6
7 8 9 10
11 12 13 14 15
```

60] Print Star Pattern.

```
* * * * *
* * * *
* * *
* *
*
```

```java
public class Program60
{
public static void main()
{
int i,j;
for(i=1;i<=5;i++)
{
for(j=5;j>=i;j--)
{
System.out.print(" * ");
```

```
}
System.out.println();
}
}
}
```

Program Output

```
* * * * *

* * * *

* * *

* *

*
```

✿✿✿

61] Print Alphabets Pattern.

```
A
B C
D E F
G H I J
K L M N O
public class Program61
{
public static void main()
{
int i,j;
char ch='A';
for(i=1;i<=5;i++)
{
for(j=1;j<=i;j++)
{
System.out.print(" "+ch);
ch++;
}
System.out.println();
```

```
}
}
```

Program Output

```
A
B C
D E F
G H I J
K L M N O
```

62] Print Alphabets Pattern.

```
A
B B
C C C
D D D D
E E E E E
public class Program62
{
public static void main()
{
int i,j;
char ch='A';
for(i=1;i<=5;i++)
{
for(j=1;j<=i;j++)
{
System.out.print(" "+ch);
}
System.out.println();
ch++;
}
}
}
```

Program Output

```
A
B B
C C C
D D D D
E E E E
```

63] Print Alphabets Pattern.

```
A B C D E
F G H I
J K L
M N
O
```

```java
public class Program63
{
public static void main()
{
int i,j;
char ch='A';
for(i=1;i<=5;i++)
{
for(j=5;j>=i;j--)
{
System.out.print(" "+ch);
ch++;
}
System.out.println();
}
}
}
```

Program Output

```
A B C D E
```

```
F G H I
J K L
M N
O
```

64] Print Alphabets Pattern.

```
A A A A A
B B B B
C C C
D D
E
public class Program64
{
public static void main()
{
int i,j;
char ch='A';
for(i=1;i<=5;i++)
{
for(j=5;j>=i;j--)
{
System.out.print(" "+ch);
}
System.out.println();
ch++;
}
}
}
```

Program Output

```
A A A A A
B B B B
C C C
```

D D
E

65] Print Alphabets Pattern.

```
A
A B
A B C
A B C D
A B C D E
public class Program65
{
public static void main()
{
char i,j;
for(i=65;i<=69;i++)
{
for(j=65;j<=i;j++)
{
System.out.print(" "+j);
}
System.out.println();
}
}
}
```

Program Output

```
A
A B
A B C
A B C D
A B C D E
```

66] Print Alphabets Pattern.

```
A
B A
C B A
D C B A
E D C B A
```

```java
public class Program66
{
public static void main()
{
char i,j;
for(i=65;i<=69;i++)
{
for(j=i;j>=65;j--)
{
System.out.print(" "+j);
}
System.out.println();
}
}
}
```

Program Output

```
A
B A
C B A
D C B A
E D C B A
```

67] Print Alphabets Pattern.

```
E D C B A
D C B A
C B A
```

B A
A

```
public class Program67
{
public static void main()
{
char i,j;
for(i=69;i>=65;i--)
{
for(j=i;j>=65;j--)
{
System.out.print(" "+j);
}
System.out.println();
}
}
}
```

Program Output

E D C B A
D C B A
C B A
B A
A

68] **Print Digit Pattern.**

1 2 3 4 5
1 2 3 4
1 2 3
1 2
1

```
public class Program68
{
```

```java
public static void main()
{
int i,j;
for(i=5;i>=1;i--)
{
for(j=1;j<=i;j++)
{
System.out.print(" "+j);
}
System.out.println();
}
}
}
```

Program Output

```
1 2 3 4 5
1 2 3 4
1 2 3
1 2
1
```

69] **Print Digit Pattern.**

```
1
1 2
1 2 3
1 2 3 4
1 2 3 4 5
1 2 3 4
1 2 3
1 2
1
```

```java
public class Program69
{
```

```java
public static void main()
{
int i,j;
for(i=1;i<=5;i++)
{
for(j=1;j<=i;j++)
{
System.out.print(" "+j);
}
System.out.println();
}
for(i=4;i>=1;i--)
{
for(j=1;j<=i;j++)
{
System.out.print(" "+j);
}
System.out.println();
}
}
}
```

Program Output

```
1
1 2
1 2 3
1 2 3 4
1 2 3 4 5
1 2 3 4
1 2 3
1 2
1
```

70] Print Digit Pattern.

```
1
2 2
3 3 3
4 4 4 4
5 5 5 5 5
4 4 4 4
3 3 3
2 2
1
```

```java
public class Program70
{
public static void main()
{
int i,j;
for(i=1;i<=5;i++)
{
for(j=1;j<=i;j++)
{
System.out.print(" "+i);
}
System.out.println();
}
for(i=4;i>=1;i--)
{
for(j=1;j<=i;j++)
{
System.out.print(" "+i);
}
System.out.println();
}
}
}
```

Program Output

```
1
2 2
3 3 3
4 4 4 4
5 5 5 5 5
4 4 4 4
3 3 3
2 2
1
```

71] Print Digit Pattern.

```
1
1 1
1 1 1
1 1 1 1
1 1 1 1 1
public class Program71
{
public static void main()
{
int i,j,k=1;
for(i=1;i<=5;i++)
{
for(j=1;j<=i;j++)
{
System.out.print(" "+k);
}
System.out.println();
}
}
}
```

Program Output

1
1 1
1 1 1
1 1 1 1
1 1 1 1 1

CHAPTER SEVEN

Sum Of Series

72] Calculate sum of series 1+2+3+4+________+100.

```
public class Program72
{
public static void main()
{
int n=1,sum=0;
while(n<=100)
{
sum=sum+n;
n++;
}
System.out.println("Sum of Series is :- "+sum);
}
}
```

Program Output

Sum of Series is :- 5050

73] Calculate sum of series 1!+2!+3!+....+10!.

```
public class Program73
{
public static void main()
{
```

```
int n,i,j;
long fact=1,sum=0;
for(j=1;j<=10;j++)
{
fact=1;
for(i=1;i<=j;i++)
fact=fact*i;
sum=sum+fact;
System.out.println("Factorial of "+j+" is "+fact);
}
for(i=1;i<=10;i++)
{
System.out.print(i+"!+");
}
System.out.print("= "+sum);
}
}
```

Program Output

Factorial of 1 is 1

Factorial of 2 is 2

Factorial of 3 is 6

Factorial of 4 is 24

Factorial of 5 is 120

Factorial of 6 is 720

Factorial of 7 is 5040

Factorial of 8 is 40320

Factorial of 9 is 362880

Factorial of 10 is 3628800

1!+2!+3!+4!+5!+6!+7!+8!+9!+10!+= 4037913

74] Print series 2 -4 6 -8 10 -12 14.....20.

```
public class Program74
```

```
{
public static void main()
{
int n,i,j;
n=2;
i=-2;
while(n<20)
{
System.out.println(n);
n=-n+i;
i=-i;
}
}
}
```

Program Output

```
2
-4
6
-8
10
-12
14
-16
18
-20
```

❧❧❧

75] Calculate sum of nth multiple of given no p.

```
import java.util.*;
public class Program75
{
public static void main()
{
```

```
int n,i,sum=0,p;
Scanner scnObj = new Scanner(System.in);
System.out.println("Enter number :- ");
p = scnObj.nextInt();
System.out.println("Enter number :- ");
n = scnObj.nextInt();
for(i=1;i<=n;i++)
sum=sum+(i*p);
System.out.println("Sum of "+n+" multiple of "+p+" is "+sum);
    }
}
```

Program Output

Enter number :-

75

Enter number :-

90

Sum of 90 multiple of 75 is 307125

CHAPTER EIGHT

Switch Statement

76] Check vowels using Switch Case Statement.

```java
import java.util.*;
public class Program76
{
public static void main()
{
char ch;
Scanner scnObj = new Scanner(System.in);
System.out.println("Enter number :- ");
ch = scnObj.next().charAt(0);
switch(ch)
{
case 'a':
case 'A':
case 'e':
case 'E':
case 'i':
case 'I':
case 'o':
case 'O':
case 'u':
case 'U':
System.out.println(ch+" is a vowel.");
```

```
break;
default:
System.out.println(ch+" is not a vowel.");
}
}
}
```

Program Output

```
Enter character :-
b
b is not a vowel.
```

<hr>

77] Convert numbers into words.

```
import java.util.*;
public class Program77
{
public static void main()
{
int ch;
Scanner scnObj = new Scanner(System.in);
System.out.println("Enter number between 1 To 10.");
ch = scnObj.nextInt();
switch(ch)
{
case 1:
System.out.println("One");
break;
case 2:
System.out.println("Two");
break;
case 3:
System.out.println("Three");
break;
```

```
case 4:
System.out.println("Four");
break;
case 5:
System.out.println("Five");
break;
case 6:
System.out.println("Six");
break;
case 7:
System.out.println("Seven");
break;
case 8:
System.out.println("Eight");
break;
case 9:
System.out.println("Nine");
break;
case 10:
System.out.println("Ten");
break;
case 0:
System.out.println("exit");
break;
}
}
}
```

Program Output

```
Enter number between 1 To 10.
7
Seven
```

78] Print Day name from week days by day number using switch case.

```java
import java.util.*;
public class Program78
{
public static void main()
{
int ch;
Scanner scnObj = new Scanner(System.in);
System.out.println("Enter number between 1 To 7.");
ch = scnObj.nextInt();
switch(ch)
{
case 1:
System.out.println("Monday");
break;
case 2:
System.out.println("Tuesday");
break;
case 3:
System.out.println("Wednesday");
break;
case 4:
System.out.println("Thursday");
break;
case 5:
System.out.println("Friday");
break;
case 6:
System.out.println("Saturday");
break;
case 7:
System.out.println("Sunday");
```

```
break;
default:
System.out.println("Enter valid choice.");
break;
}
}
}
```

Program Output

Enter number between 1 To 7.

5

Friday

❧❧❧

79] Print color name from colors list using switch case.

```
import java.util.*;
public class Program79
{
public static void main()
{
int ch;
Scanner scnObj = new Scanner(System.in);
System.out.println("Enter number between 1 To 7.");
ch = scnObj.nextInt();
switch(ch)
{
case 1:
System.out.println("Red");
break;
case 2:
System.out.println("Orange");
break;
case 3:
System.out.println("Green");
```

```
break;
case 4:
System.out.println("Blue");
break;
case 5:
System.out.println("Violet");
break;
case 6:
System.out.println("Black");
break;
case 7:
System.out.println("White");
break;
case 8:
System.out.println("Pink");
break;
default:
System.out.println("Enter valid choice.");
break;
}
}
}
```

Program Output

```
Enter number between 1 To 7.
2
Orange
```

CHAPTER NINE

Single Dimensional Array

80] Find maximum no from given array.

```java
import java.util.*;
public class Program81
{
public static void main()
{
int i,max=0,min=1,n;
int arr[] = new int[10];
Scanner scnObj = new Scanner(System.in);
System.out.println("Enter number of elements :-");
n = scnObj.nextInt();
System.out.println("Enter "+n+" elements");
for(i=1;i<=n;i++)
{
arr[i] = scnObj.nextInt();
}
for(i=1;i<=n;i++)
{
if(arr[i] < min)
min = arr[i];
if(arr[i] > max)
```

```
max = arr[i];
}
System.out.println("The element "+max+" is maximum
no.");
System.out.println("The element "+min+" is minimum
no.");
}
}
```

Program Output

Enter number of elements :-

4

Enter 4 elements

70

65

47

89

The element 89 is maximum no.

❧❧❧

81] Find smallest and largest no from 10 nos.

```
import java.util.*;
public class Program81
{
public static void main()
{
int i,max=0,n;
int arr[] = new int[10];
int min = Integer.MAX_VALUE;
Scanner scnObj = new Scanner(System.in);
System.out.println("Enter number of elements :-");
n = scnObj.nextInt();
System.out.println("Enter "+n+" elements");
for(i=1;i<=n;i++)
```

```
{
arr[i] = scnObj.nextInt();
}
for(i=1;i<=n;i++)
{
if(arr[i] < min)
min = arr[i];
if(arr[i] > max)
max = arr[i];
}
System.out.println("The element "+max+" is maximum
no.");
System.out.println("The element "+min+" is minimum
no.");
}
}
```

Program Output

Enter number of elements :-
7
Enter 7 elements
45
60
79
82
34
98
56
The element 98 is maximum no.
The element 34 is minimum no.

❦❦❦

82] Search number from user input at runtime.

```
import java.util.*;
```

```java
public class Program82
{
public static void main()
{
int sernum=0,cnt=0,i;
int n[] = new int[5];
Scanner scnObj = new Scanner(System.in);
System.out.println("Enter the five element :-");
for(i=0;i<5;i++)
{
n[i] = scnObj.nextInt();
}
System.out.println("Enter the no to search :-");
sernum = scnObj.nextInt();
for(i=0;i<5;i++)
{
if(sernum==n[i])
cnt++;
}
if(cnt==0)
System.out.println("No not found.");
else
System.out.println("The   number   found   in   "+cnt+"
times");
}
}
```

Program Output

Enter the five element :-

68

89

36

72

19

Enter the no to search :-
72
The number found in 1 times

83] Calculate sum of element & average of one-dimensional array.

```java
import java.util.*;
public class Program83
{
public static void main()
{
int i,sum=0,n;
int arr[] = new int[10];
float avg=0;
Scanner scnObj = new Scanner(System.in);
System.out.println("Enter no of elements :-");
n = scnObj.nextInt();
System.out.println("Enter elements :-");
for(i=1;i<=n;i++)
{
arr[i] = scnObj.nextInt();
}
for(i=1;i<=n;i++)
{
sum=sum+arr[i];
avg=(float)sum/n;
}
System.out.println("The sum of elements :-"+sum);
System.out.println("Average of elements :-"+avg);
}
}
```

Program Output

Enter no of elements :-
8
Enter elements :-
67
80
47
25
67
81
73
50
The sum of elements :-490
Average of elements :-61.25

84] Print one dimensional array.

```
import java.util.*;
public class Program84
{
public static void main()
{
int i,arr[] = new int[10];
Scanner scnObj = new Scanner(System.in);
System.out.println("Enter 5 elements :-");
for(i=1;i<=5;i++)
{
arr[i] = scnObj.nextInt();
}
System.out.println("Array elements ");
for(i=1;i<=5;i++)
{
System.out.println(arr[i]);
}
```

```
}
}
```

Program Output

```
Enter 5 elements :-
67
83
41
69
18
Array elements
67
83
41
69
18
```

85] Sort one dimensional array in an ascending order.

```
import java.util.*;
public class Program85
{
public static void main()
{
int i,j,temp,arr[] = new int[10];
Scanner scnObj = new Scanner(System.in);
System.out.println("Enter 5 elements :-");
for(i=0;i<5;i++)
{
arr[i] = scnObj.nextInt();
}
for(i=0;i<5;i++)
{
for(j=0;j<5;j++)
```

```
{
if(arr[i]<arr[j])
{
temp = arr[i];
arr[i] = arr[j];
arr[j] = temp;
}
}
}
System.out.println("Sorted Array In Ascending orde:-
");
for(j=0;j<5;j++)
{
System.out.println(arr[j]);
}
}
}
```

Program Output

Enter 5 elements :-

56

78

29

61

45

Sorted Array In Ascending order:-

29

45

56

61

78

86] Sort one dimensional array in descending order.

```java
import java.util.*;
public class Program86
{
public static void main()
{
int i,j,temp,arr[] = new int[10];
Scanner scnObj = new Scanner(System.in);
System.out.println("Enter 5 elements :-");
for(i=0;i<5;i++)
{
arr[i] = scnObj.nextInt();
}
for(i=0;i<5;i++)
{
for(j=0;j<5;j++)
{
if(arr[i]>arr[j])
{
temp = arr[i];
arr[i] = arr[j];
arr[j] = temp;
}
}
}
System.out.println("Sorted Array in descending order:-");
for(j=0;j<5;j++)
{
System.out.println(arr[j]);
}
}
}
```

Program Output

Enter 5 elements :-
37
62
89
25
91
Sorted Array in descending order:-
91
89
62
37
25

87] Print array elements in reverse order.

```java
import java.util.*;
public class Program87
{
public static void main()
{
int n, i, d, temp, x[] = new int[100],y[] = new int[100];
Scanner scnObj = new Scanner(System.in);
System.out.println("Enter number of elements in array :-");
n = scnObj.nextInt();
System.out.println("Enter "+n+" numbers");
for(i=0;i<n;i++)
{
x[i] = scnObj.nextInt();
}
for ( i = n - 1, d = 0 ; i >= 0 ; i--, d++ )
y[d] = x[i];
for ( i = 0 ; i < n ; i++ )
```

```java
x[i] = y[i];
System.out.println("Array in reverse order :-");
for( i = 0 ; i < n ; i++ )
System.out.println(x[i]);
}
}
```

Program Output

Enter number of elements in array :-

4

Enter 4 numbers

78

27

84

56

Array in reverse order :-

56

84

27

78

❧❧❧

88] Search element using linear search.

```java
import java.util.*;
public class Program88
{
public static void main()
{
int find, i,loc=0, num,x[] = new int[100];
Scanner scnObj = new Scanner(System.in);
System.out.println("Enter number of elements in array :-");
num = scnObj.nextInt();
System.out.println("Enter "+num+" numbers");
```

```
for(i=0;i<num;i++)
{
x[i] = scnObj.nextInt();
}
System.out.println("Enter number to search");
find = scnObj.nextInt();
for ( i = 0 ; i < num ; i++ )
{
if ( x[i] == find )
{
loc = i+1;
System.out.println(find+" is present at location "+loc);
break;
}
}
if ( i == num )
System.out.println(find+" is present at location "+i+1);
}
}
```

Program Output

Enter number of elements in array :-

4

Enter 4 numbers

78

27

84

56

Array in reverse order :-

56

84

27

78

89] Search multiple occurrences of element using linear search.

```java
import java.util.*;
public class Program89
{
public static void main()
{
int find, i=0, loc, cnt=0, num,x[] = new int[100];
Scanner scnObj = new Scanner(System.in);
System.out.println("Enter number of elements in array :-");
num = scnObj.nextInt();
System.out.println("Enter "+num+" numbers");
for(i=0;i<num;i++)
{
x[i] = scnObj.nextInt();
}
System.out.println("Enter number to search");
find = scnObj.nextInt();
for ( i = 0 ; i < num ; i++ )
{
if ( x[i] == find )
{
loc = i+1;
System.out.println(find+" is present at location "+loc);
cnt++;
}
}
if ( cnt == 0 )
{
System.out.println(find+" is not present in array");
}
```

```
else
{
System.out.println(find+" is present in array "+cnt+"
times");
}
}
}
```

Program Output

Enter number of elements in array :-

4

Enter 4 numbers

56

72

34

19

Enter number to search

34

34 is present at location 3

34 is present in array 1 times

90] Search element using binary Search.

```
import java.util.*;
public class Program90
{
public static void main()
{
int n,i,find,bgn,end,mid,loc=0, x[] = new int[100];
Scanner scnObj = new Scanner(System.in);
System.out.println("Enter number of elements in array
:-");
n = scnObj.nextInt();
System.out.println("Enter "+n+" numbers");
```

```
for(i=0;i<n;i++)
{
x[i] = scnObj.nextInt();
}
System.out.println("Enter number to search");
find = scnObj.nextInt();
bgn = 0;
end = n - 1;
mid = (bgn+end)/2;
while( bgn<= end )
{
if (x[mid] < find )
bgn = mid + 1;
else if ( x[mid] == find )
{
loc=mid+1;
System.out.println(find+" found at location "+loc);
break;
}
else
end = mid - 1;
mid = (bgn + end)/2;
}
if ( bgn> end )
System.out.println("Not found! "+find+" not present in array.");
}
}
```

Program Output

Enter number of elements in array :-

6

Enter 6 numbers

75

```
49
26
68
92
26
Enter number to search
26
26 found at location 3
```

91] Sorting method Bubble sort.

```
import java.util.*;
public class Program91
{
public static void main()
{
int x[] = new int[100], no, i, d, temp;
Scanner scnObj = new Scanner(System.in);
System.out.println("Enter number of elements in array :-");
no = scnObj.nextInt();
System.out.println("Enter "+no+" numbers");
for(i=0;i<no;i++)
{
x[i] = scnObj.nextInt();
}
for ( i = 0 ; i < ( no - 1 ) ; i++ )
{
for ( d = 0 ; d < no - i - 1 ; d++ )
{
if ( x[d] > x[d+1] )
{
temp = x[d];
```

```
x[d] = x[d+1];
x[d+1] = temp;
}
}
}
System.out.println("Sorted List in ascending order.");
for(i=0;i<no;i++)
{
System.out.println(x[i]);
}
}
}
```

Program Output

Enter number of elements in array :-

5

Enter 5 numbers

43

87

23

57

13

Sorted List in ascending order.

13

23

43

57

87

⚜⚜⚜

92] Sorting method Insertion sort.

```
import java.util.*;
public class Program92
{
```

```java
public static void main()
{
int x[] = new int[100], no, i, d, temp, k;
Scanner scnObj = new Scanner(System.in);
System.out.println("Enter number of elements in array :-");
no = scnObj.nextInt();
System.out.println("Enter "+no+" numbers");
for(i=0;i<no;i++)
{
x[i] = scnObj.nextInt();
}
for ( i = 1 ; i <= no - 1 ; i++ )
{
for ( d = 0 ; d <= i - 1 ; d++ )
{
if ( x[i] < x[d] )
{
temp = x[d];
x[d] = x[i];
for ( k = i ; k > d ; k-- )
x[k] = x[k-1];
x[k+1] = temp;
}
}
}
System.out.println("Sorted List in ascending order.");
for(i=0;i<no;i++)
{
System.out.println(x[i]);
}
}
}
```

Program Output

Enter number of elements in array :-

5

Enter 5 numbers

34

76

23

89

11

Sorted List in ascending order.

11

23

34

76

89

93] Sorting method Selection sort.

```java
import java.util.*;
public class Program93
{
public static void main()
{
int x[] = new int[100],temp, no, i, d;
Scanner scnObj = new Scanner(System.in);
System.out.println("Enter number of elements in array :-");
no = scnObj.nextInt();
System.out.println("Enter "+no+" numbers");
for(i=0;i<no;i++)
{
x[i] = scnObj.nextInt();
}
```

```
for ( i = 0 ; i < ( no - 1) ; i++ )
{
for ( d = ( i + 1 ) ; d <= ( no - 1 ) ; d++ )
{
if ( x[i] > x[d] )
{
temp = x[i];
x[i] = x[d];
x[d] = temp;
}
}
}
System.out.println("Sorted List in ascending order.");
for(i=0;i<no;i++)
{
System.out.println(x[i]);
}
}
}
```

Program Output

Enter number of elements in array :-
5
Enter 5 numbers
98
45
23
88
40
Sorted List in ascending bling order.
23
40
45
88

98

94] Get number's find even, odd & sum of them.

```java
import java.util.*;
public class Program94
{
public static void main()
{
int i,arr[] = new int[100],evensum=0,oddsum=0,n;
Scanner scnObj = new Scanner(System.in);
System.out.println("Enter number of elements in array :-");
n = scnObj.nextInt();
System.out.println("Enter "+n+" numbers");
for(i=0;i<n;i++)
{
arr[i] = scnObj.nextInt();
}
for(i=0;i<n;i++)
{
if(arr[i]%2==0)
{
System.out.println(arr[i]+" is even no.");
evensum=evensum+arr[i];
}
else
{
System.out.println(arr[i]+" is odd no.");
oddsum=oddsum+arr[i];
}
}
```

```
    System.out.println("The    sum    of    even    numbers
"+evensum);
    System.out.println("The    sum    of    odd    numbers
"+oddsum);
    }
}
```

Enter number of elements in array :-

6

Enter 6 numbers

65

34

87

23

45

78

65 is odd no.

34 is even no.

87 is odd no.

23 is odd no.

45 is odd no.

78 is even no.

The sum of even numbers 112

The sum of odd numbers 220

95] Copy one array into another array in the reverse order.

```
import java.util.*;
public class Program95
{
public static void main()
{
int i,j,arr1[] = new int[100], arr2[] = new int[100];
```

```java
Scanner scnObj = new Scanner(System.in);
System.out.println("Enter 10 numbers");
for(i=0;i<=9;i++)
{
arr1[i] = scnObj.nextInt();
}
for(i=0,j=9;i<=9;i++,j--)
arr2[j]=arr1[i];
System.out.println("Elements in reverse order.");
for(j=0;j<=9;j++)
{
System.out.println(arr2[j]);
}
}
}
```

Program Output

Enter 10 numbers
56
45
78
76
66
23
45
98
54
12
Elements in reverse order.
12
54
98
45
23

66
76
78
45
56

CHAPTER TEN

Two Dimensional Array

96] Print the matrix (two-dimensional array)
```
import java.util.*;
public class Program96
{
public static void main()
{
int i,j,r,c;
int mat[][] = new int[5][5];
Scanner scnObj = new Scanner(System.in);
System.out.println("Enter no of rows:");
r = scnObj.nextInt();
System.out.println("Enter no of columns:");
c = scnObj.nextInt();
System.out.println("Enter "+r+"x"+c+" Matrix");
for(i=0;i<r;i++)
{
for(j=0;j<c;j++)
{
mat[i][j] = scnObj.nextInt();
}
}
System.out.println("Given Matrix is :-");
for(i=0;i<r;i++)
```

```
{
for(j=0;j<c;j++)
{
System.out.print("\t"+mat[i][j]);
}
System.out.println();
}
}
}
```

Program Output

Enter no of rows:

3

Enter no of columns:

3

Enter 3x3 Matrix

1

2

3

4

5

6

7

8

9

Given Matrix is :-

1 2 3

4 5 6

7 8 9

97] Search number from matrix.

```
import java.util.*;
public class Program97
```

```java
{
public static void main()
{
int i,j,r,c,num,cnt=0;
int mat[][] = new int[5][5];
Scanner scnObj = new Scanner(System.in);
System.out.println("Enter no of rows:");
r = scnObj.nextInt();
System.out.println("Enter no of columns:");
c = scnObj.nextInt();
System.out.println("Enter "+r+"x"+c+" Matrix");
for(i=0;i<r;i++)
{
for(j=0;j<c;j++)
{
mat[i][j] = scnObj.nextInt();
}
}
System.out.println("Enter no to search :-");
num = scnObj.nextInt();
for(i=0;i<r;i++)
{
for(j=0;j<c;j++)
{
if(num == mat[i][j])
{
cnt++;
}
}
}
if(cnt == 0)
System.out.println("Number is not found in matrix.");
else
```

```
    System.out.println("Number is found in matrix "+cnt+"
times");
    }
}
```

Program Output

Enter no of rows:

3

Enter no of columns:

3

Enter 3x3 Matrix

1

2

3

4

5

6

9

8

7

Enter no to search :-

5

Number is found in matrix 1 times

98] Perform operation addition of two matrices.

```
import java.util.*;
public class Program98
{
public static void main()
{
int i,j;
int a[][] = new int[5][5];
int b[][] = new int[5][5];
```

```java
int c[][] = new int[5][5];
Scanner scnObj = new Scanner(System.in);
System.out.println("Enter First 3 X 3 Matrix");
for(i=0;i<3;i++)
{
for(j=0;j<3;j++)
{
a[i][j] = scnObj.nextInt();
}
}
System.out.println("Enter Second 3 X 3 Matrix");
for(i=0;i<3;i++)
{
for(j=0;j<3;j++)
{
b[i][j] = scnObj.nextInt();
}
}
System.out.println("Addition of Matrices is");
for(i=0;i<3;i++)
{
for(j=0;j<3;j++)
{
c[i][j] = a[i][j] + b[i][j];
System.out.print("\t"+c[i][j]);
}
System.out.println();
}
}
}
```

Program Output

Enter First 3 X 3 Matrix

5

6
7
4
3
2
8
9
1
Enter Second 3 X 3 Matrix
2
3
4
5
6
9
8
7
1
Addition of Matrices is
7 9 11
9 9 11
16 16 2

99] Program to find minimum no from two dimensional array.

```java
import java.util.*;
public class Program99
{
public static void main()
{
int i,j,min;
int mat[][] = new int[5][5];
```

```java
Scanner scnObj = new Scanner(System.in);
System.out.println("Enter 3 x 3 Matrix");
for(i=0;i<3;i++)
{
for(j=0;j<3;j++)
{
mat[i][j] = scnObj.nextInt();
}
}
min = mat[0][0];
for(i=0;i<3;i++)
{
for(j=0;j<3;j++)
{
if(mat[i][j]<min)
min=mat[i][j];
}
}
System.out.println("The minimum number from matrix is "+min);
}
}
```

Program Output

Enter 3 x 3 Matrix

45

65

76

34

56

24

89

60

67

The minimum number from matrix is 24

100] Program to find largest no from 3*3 matrix.

```java
import java.util.*;
public class Program100
{
public static void main()
{
int i,j,max;
int mat[][] = new int[5][5];
Scanner scnObj = new Scanner(System.in);
System.out.println("Enter 3 x 3 Matrix");
for(i=0;i<3;i++)
{
for(j=0;j<3;j++)
{
mat[i][j] = scnObj.nextInt();
}
}
max = mat[0][0];
for(i=0;i<3;i++)
{
for(j=0;j<3;j++)
{
if(mat[i][j]>max)
max=mat[i][j];
}
}
System.out.println("The largest number from matrix is "+max);
}
}
```

Program Output

Enter 3 x 3 Matrix

79

86

99

23

54

83

66

47

53

The largest number from matrix is 99

101] Program to Sort two dimensional array.

```java
import java.util.*;
public class Program101
{
public static void main()
{
int i,j,k=0,temp;
int a[][] = new int[5][5],b[] = new int[9];
Scanner scnObj = new Scanner(System.in);
System.out.println("Enter 3 x 3 Matrix");
for(i=0;i<3;i++)
{
for(j=0;j<3;j++)
{
a[i][j] = scnObj.nextInt();
b[k]=a[i][j];
k++;
}
}
```

```
for(i=0;i<9;i++)
{
for(j=i+1;j<9;j++)
{
if(b[i]>b[j])
{
temp = b[i];
b[i] = b[j];
b[j] = temp;
}
}
}
k=0;
System.out.println("Sorted Matrix is");
for(i=0;i<3;i++)
{
for(j=0;j<3;j++)
{
a[i][j]=b[k];
System.out.print("\t"+a[i][j]);
k++;
}
System.out.println();
}
}
}
```

Program Output

Enter 3 x 3 Matrix

56

35

48

76

98

82
27
66
23
Sorted Matrix is
23 27 35
48 56 66
76 82 98

102] Program to print even no from two dimensional array.

```java
import java.util.*;
public class Program102
{
public static void main()
{
int i,j,r,c;
int mat[][] = new int[5][5];
Scanner scnObj = new Scanner(System.in);
System.out.println("Enter no of rows:");
r = scnObj.nextInt();
System.out.println("Enter no of columns:");
c = scnObj.nextInt();
System.out.println("Enter "+r+"x"+c+" Matrix");
for(i=0;i<r;i++)
{
for(j=0;j<c;j++)
{
mat[i][j] = scnObj.nextInt();
}
}
System.out.println("Given Matrix is :-");
```

```
for(i=0;i<r;i++)
{
for(j=0;j<c;j++)
{
System.out.print("\t"+mat[i][j]);
}
System.out.println();
}
System.out.println("Even numbers are");
for(i=0;i<r;i++)
{
for(j=0;j<c;j++)
{
if(mat[i][j]%2==0)
System.out.print("\t"+mat[i][j]);
}
}
}
}
```

Program Output

Enter no of rows:

3

Enter no of columns:

3

Enter 3x3 Matrix

78

98

70

47

65

79

86

34

```
56
Given Matrix is :-
78 98 70
47 65 79
86 34 56
Even numbers are
78 98 70 86 34 56
```

103] Program to print odd no from two dimensional array.

```java
import java.util.*;
public class Program103
{
public static void main()
{
int i,j,r,c;
int mat[][] = new int[5][5];
Scanner scnObj = new Scanner(System.in);
System.out.println("Enter no of rows:");
r = scnObj.nextInt();
System.out.println("Enter no of columns:");
c = scnObj.nextInt();
System.out.println("Enter "+r+"x"+c+" Matrix");
for(i=0;i<r;i++)
{
for(j=0;j<c;j++)
{
mat[i][j] = scnObj.nextInt();
}
}
System.out.println("Given Matrix is :-");
for(i=0;i<r;i++)
```

```
{
for(j=0;j<c;j++)
{
System.out.print("\t"+mat[i][j]);
}
System.out.println();
}
System.out.println("Odd numbers are");
for(i=0;i<r;i++)
{
for(j=0;j<c;j++)
{
if(mat[i][j]%2!=0)
System.out.print("\t"+mat[i][j]);
}
}
}
}
```

Program Output

Enter no of rows:

3

Enter no of columns:

3

Enter 3x3 Matrix

7

6

34

56

23

89

77

53

29

Given Matrix is :-
7 6 34
56 23 89
77 53 29
Odd numbers are
7 23 89 77 53 29

104] Program to print prime no from two dimensional array.

```
import java.util.*;
public class Program104
{
public static void main()
{
int i,j,k,r,c,fact=0;
int mat[][] = new int[5][5];
Scanner scnObj = new Scanner(System.in);
System.out.println("Enter no of rows:");
r = scnObj.nextInt();
System.out.println("Enter no of columns:");
c = scnObj.nextInt();
System.out.println("Enter "+r+"x"+c+" Matrix");
for(i=0;i<r;i++)
{
for(j=0;j<c;j++)
{
mat[i][j] = scnObj.nextInt();
}
}
System.out.println("Given Matrix is :-");
for(i=0;i<r;i++)
{
```

```java
for(j=0;j<c;j++)
{
System.out.print("\t"+mat[i][j]);
}
System.out.println();
}
System.out.println("Prime numbers are");
for(i=0;i<r;i++)
{
for(j=0;j<c;j++)
{
fact=0;
for(k=1;k<=mat[i][j];k++)
{
if(mat[i][j]%k==0)
fact++;
}
if(fact==2)
System.out.print("\t"+mat[i][j]);
}
}
}
}
```

Program Output

Enter no of rows:

3

Enter no of columns:

3

Enter 3x3 Matrix

23

56

78

89

```
53
67
73
7
31
Given Matrix is :-
23 56 78
89 53 67
73 7 31
Prime numbers are
23 89 53 67 73 7 31
```

105] Program to calculate two dimensional matrix multiplications.

```java
import java.util.*;
public class Program105
{
public static void main()
{
int i,j,k,sum = 0;
int a[ ][ ] = new int[5][5];
int b[ ][ ] = new int[5][5];
int c[ ][ ] = new int[5][5];
Scanner scnObj = new Scanner(System.in);
System.out.println("Enter First 3 X 3 Matrix");
for(i=0;i<3;i++)
{
for(j=0;j<3;j++)
{
a[i][j] = scnObj.nextInt();
}
}
```

```java
System.out.println("Enter Second 3 X 3 Matrix");
for(i=0;i<3;i++)
{
for(j=0;j<3;j++)
{
b[i][j] = scnObj.nextInt();
}
}
System.out.println("Multiplication of Matrices is");
for(i=0;i<3;i++)
{
for(j=0;j<3;j++)
{
for(k=0;k<3;k++)
{
sum = sum + a[i][k]*b[k][j];
}
c[i][j] = sum;
sum = 0;
}
}
for(i=0;i<3;i++)
{
for(j=0;j<3;j++)
{
System.out.print("\t"+c[i][j]);
}
System.out.println();
}
}
}
```

Program Output

Enter First 3 X 3 Matrix

1
2
3
4
5
6
7
8
9
Enter Second 3 X 3 Matrix
9
8
7
6
5
4
3
2
1
Multiplication of Matrices is
30 24 18
84 69 54
138 114 90

106] Program to print Transpose Of matrix

```
import java.util.*;
public class Program106
{
public static void main()
{
int i,j,r,c;
int mat[][] = new int[5][5];
```

```java
Scanner scnObj = new Scanner(System.in);
System.out.println("Enter no of rows:");
r = scnObj.nextInt();
System.out.println("Enter no of columns:");
c = scnObj.nextInt();
System.out.println("Enter "+r+"x"+c+" Matrix");
for(i=0;i<r;i++)
{
for(j=0;j<c;j++)
{
mat[i][j] = scnObj.nextInt();
}
}
System.out.println("Given Matrix is :-");
for(i=0;i<r;i++)
{
for(j=0;j<c;j++)
{
System.out.print("\t"+mat[i][j]);
}
System.out.println();
}
System.out.println("Transpose Of Matrix is :-");
for(i=0;i<r;i++)
{
for(j=0;j<c;j++)
{
System.out.print("\t"+mat[j][i]);
}
System.out.println();
}
}
}
```

Program Output

Enter no of rows:

3

Enter no of columns:

3

Enter 3x3 Matrix

7

8

9

1

2

3

4

5

6

Given Matrix is :-

7 8 9

1 2 3

4 5 6

Transpose Of Matrix is :-

7 1 4

8 2 5

9 3 6

107] Print the upper triangular matrix.

```java
import java.util.*;
public class Program107
{
public static void main()
{
int i,j;
int mat[][] = new int[5][5];
```

```
System.out.println("Upper Triangular Matrix is :-");
for(i=0;i<3;i++)
{
for(j=0;j<3;j++)
{
if(i<=j)
mat[i][j]=1;
else
mat[i][j]=0;
System.out.print("\t"+mat[i][j]);
}
System.out.println();
}
}
}
```

Program Output

```
Upper Triangular Matrix is :-
1 1 1
0 1 1
0 0 1
```

108] Calculate sum of upper triangular matrix.

```
import java.util.*;
public class Program108
{
public static void main()
{
int i,j,r,c,sum=0;
int mat[][] = new int[5][5];
Scanner scnObj = new Scanner(System.in);
System.out.println("Enter no of rows:");
r = scnObj.nextInt();
```

```java
System.out.println("Enter no of columns:");
c = scnObj.nextInt();
System.out.println("Enter "+r+"x"+c+" Matrix");
for(i=0;i<r;i++)
{
for(j=0;j<c;j++)
{
mat[i][j] = scnObj.nextInt();
}
}
System.out.println("Given Matrix is :-");
for(i=0;i<r;i++)
{
for(j=0;j<c;j++)
{
System.out.print("\t"+mat[i][j]);
}
System.out.println();
}
for(i=0;i<r;i++)
{
for(j=0;j<c;j++)
{
if(j>=i)
sum+=mat[i][j];
}
}
System.out.println("Sum of upper triangular matrix is "+sum);
}
}
```

Program Output

Enter no of rows:

3
Enter no of columns:
3
Enter 3x3 Matrix
23
46
54
78
96
23
14
44
84
Given Matrix is :-
23 46 54
78 96 23
14 44 84
Sum of upper triangular matrix is 326

109] Find minimum no from upper triangular matrix.

```java
import java.util.*;
public class Program109
{
public static void main()
{
int i,j,r,c,sum=0;
int mat[][] = new int[5][5];
Scanner scnObj = new Scanner(System.in);
System.out.println("Enter no of rows:");
r = scnObj.nextInt();
System.out.println("Enter no of columns:");
c = scnObj.nextInt();
```

```java
System.out.println("Enter "+r+"x"+c+" Matrix");
for(i=0;i<r;i++)
{
for(j=0;j<c;j++)
{
mat[i][j] = scnObj.nextInt();
}
}
System.out.println("Given Matrix is :-");
for(i=0;i<r;i++)
{
for(j=0;j<c;j++)
{
System.out.print("\t"+mat[i][j]);
}
System.out.println();
}
for(i=0;i<r;i++)
{
for(j=0;j<c;j++)
{
if(mat[i][j]<mat[i+1][j+1])
mat[i+1][j+1]=mat[i][j];
}
}
System.out.println("Minimum   number   from   upper
triangular matrix is "+mat[0][0]);
}
}
```

Program Output

Enter no of rows:

3

Enter no of columns:

```
3
Enter 3x3 Matrix
23
54
56
76
87
89
12
32
97
Given Matrix is :-
23 54 56
76 87 89
12 32 97
Minimum number from upper triangular matrix is 23
```

110] Find maximum no from upper triangular matrix.

```java
import java.util.*;
public class Program110
{
public static void main()
{
int i,j,r,c,sum=0,big;
int mat[][] = new int[5][5];
Scanner scnObj = new Scanner(System.in);
System.out.println("Enter no of rows:");
r = scnObj.nextInt();
System.out.println("Enter no of columns:");
c = scnObj.nextInt();
System.out.println("Enter "+r+"x"+c+" Matrix");
for(i=0;i<r;i++)
```

```java
{
for(j=0;j<c;j++)
{
mat[i][j] = scnObj.nextInt();
}
}
System.out.println("Given Matrix is :-");
for(i=0;i<r;i++)
{
for(j=0;j<c;j++)
{
System.out.print("\t"+mat[i][j]);
}
System.out.println();
}
big=mat[0][0];
for(i=0;i<r;i++)
{
for(j=0;j<c;j++)
{
if(j>=i)
{
if(mat[i][j]>big)
big=mat[i][j];
}
}
}
System.out.println("Maximum   number   from   upper
triangular matrix is "+big);
}
}
```

Program Output

Enter no of rows:

3
Enter no of columns:
3
Enter 3x3 Matrix
76
45
78
23
45
86
12
44
92
Given Matrix is :-
76 45 78
23 45 86
12 44 92
Maximum number from upper triangular matrix is 92

111] Print lower triangular matrix.

```
import java.util.*;
public class Program111
{
public static void main()
{
int i,j;
int mat[][] = new int[5][5];
System.out.println("Lower Triangular Matrix is :-");
for(i=0;i<3;i++)
{
for(j=0;j<3;j++)
{
```

```
if(i>=j)
mat[i][j]=1;
else
mat[i][j]=0;
System.out.print("\t"+mat[i][j]);
}
System.out.println();
}
}
}
```

Program Output

```
Lower Triangular Matrix is :-
1 0 0
1 1 0
1 1 1
```

112] Print minimum no from lower triangular matrix.

```
import java.util.*;
public class Program112
{
public static void main()
{
int i,j,r,c,sum=0,min;
int mat[][] = new int[5][5];
Scanner scnObj = new Scanner(System.in);
System.out.println("Enter no of rows:");
r = scnObj.nextInt();
System.out.println("Enter no of columns:");
c = scnObj.nextInt();
System.out.println("Enter "+r+"x"+c+" Matrix");
for(i=0;i<r;i++)
{
```

```
for(j=0;j<c;j++)
{
mat[i][j] = scnObj.nextInt();
}
}
System.out.println("Given Matrix is :-");
for(i=0;i<r;i++)
{
for(j=0;j<c;j++)
{
System.out.print("\t"+mat[i][j]);
}
System.out.println();
}
min=mat[0][0];
for(i=0;i<r;i++)
{
for(j=0;j<c;j++)
{
if(j<=i)
{
if(mat[i][j]<min)
min=mat[i][j];
}
}
}
System.out.println("Minimum    number    from    lower
triangular matrix is "+min);
}
}
```

Program Output

```
Enter no of rows:
3
```

Enter no of columns:
3
Enter 3x3 Matrix
23
65
89
76
45
17
83
42
22
Given Matrix is :-
23 65 89
76 45 17
83 42 22
Minimum number from lower triangular matrix is 22.

113] Print maximum no from lower triangular matrix.

```
import java.util.*;
public class Program113
{
public static void main()
{
int i,j,r,c,sum=0,big;
int mat[][] = new int[5][5];
Scanner scnObj = new Scanner(System.in);
System.out.println("Enter no of rows:");
r = scnObj.nextInt();
System.out.println("Enter no of columns:");
c = scnObj.nextInt();
System.out.println("Enter "+r+"x"+c+" Matrix");
```

```
for(i=0;i<r;i++)
{
for(j=0;j<c;j++)
{
mat[i][j] = scnObj.nextInt();
}
}
System.out.println("Given Matrix is :-");
for(i=0;i<r;i++)
{
for(j=0;j<c;j++)
{
System.out.print("\t"+mat[i][j]);
}
System.out.println();
}
big=mat[0][0];
for(i=0;i<r;i++)
{
for(j=0;j<c;j++)
{
if(j<=i)
{
if(mat[i][j]>big)
big=mat[i][j];
}
}
}
System.out.println("Maximum    number    from    lower
triangular matrix is "+big);
}
}
```

Program Output

Enter no of rows:
3
Enter no of columns:
3
Enter 3x3 Matrix
14
65
34
76
87
42
93
50
26
Given Matrix is :-
14 65 34
76 87 42
93 50 26
Maximum number from lower triangular matrix is 93

114] Calculate sum of lower triangular matrix.
```
import java.util.*;
public class Program114
{
public static void main()
{
int i,j,r,c,sum=0;
int mat[][] = new int[5][5];
Scanner scnObj = new Scanner(System.in);
System.out.println("Enter no of rows:");
r = scnObj.nextInt();
System.out.println("Enter no of columns:");
```

```
c = scnObj.nextInt();
System.out.println("Enter "+r+"x"+c+" Matrix");
for(i=0;i<r;i++)
{
for(j=0;j<c;j++)
{
mat[i][j] = scnObj.nextInt();
}
}
System.out.println("Given Matrix is :-");
for(i=0;i<r;i++)
{
for(j=0;j<c;j++)
{
System.out.print("\t"+mat[i][j]);
}
System.out.println();
}
for(i=0;i<r;i++)
{
for(j=0;j<c;j++)
{
if(j<=i)
sum+=mat[i][j];
}
}
System.out.println("Sum of lower triangular matrix is "+sum);
}
}
Enter no of rows:
3
Enter no of columns:
```

3
Enter 3x3 Matrix
4
5
6
1
2
3
7
8
9
Given Matrix is :-
4 5 6
1 2 3
7 8 9
Sum of lower triangular matrix is 31

❧❧❧

115] Print the identity matrix.

```java
import java.util.*;
public class Program115
{
public static void main()
{
int i,j;
int mat[][] = new int[5][5];
System.out.println("Identity Matrix is :-");
for(i=0;i<3;i++)
{
for(j=0;j<3;j++)
{
if(i==j)
mat[i][j]=1;
```

```
else
mat[i][j]=0;
System.out.print("\t"+mat[i][j]);
}
System.out.println();
}
}
}
```

Program Output

```
Identity Matrix is :-
1 0 0
0 1 0
0 0 1
```

❧❧❧

116] Calculate and print sum of row elements.

```
import java.util.*;
public class Program116
{
public static void main()
{
int i,j,sum;
int mat[][] = new int[5][5];
Scanner scnObj = new Scanner(System.in);
System.out.println("Enter 3 X 3 Matrix");
for(i=0;i<3;i++)
{
for(j=0;j<3;j++)
{
mat[i][j] = scnObj.nextInt();
}
}
System.out.println("Given Matrix is \t\t Sum");
```

```
for(i=0;i<3;i++)
{
sum = 0;
for(j=0;j<3;j++)
{
System.out.print("\t"+mat[i][j]);
sum +=mat[i][j];
}
System.out.print("\t"+sum);
System.out.println();
}
}
}
```

Program Output

Enter 3 X 3 Matrix

34

12

25

46

58

76

98

81

63

Given Matrix is Sum

34 12 25 71

46 58 76 180

98 81 63 242

117] Calculate and print sum of column elements.

```
import java.util.*;
public class Program117
```

```java
{
public static void main()
{
int i,j,sum[] = new int[5];
int mat[][] = new int[5][5];
Scanner scnObj = new Scanner(System.in);
System.out.println("Enter 3 X 3 Matrix");
for(i=0;i<3;i++)
{
for(j=0;j<3;j++)
{
mat[i][j] = scnObj.nextInt();
}
}
System.out.println("Given Matrix is");
for(i=0;i<3;i++)
{
sum[i] = 0;
for(j=0;j<3;j++)
{
System.out.print("\t"+mat[i][j]);
sum[i] +=mat[j][i];
}
System.out.println();
}
System.out.println("Column Sum");
for(i=0;i<3;i++)
{
System.out.print("\t"+sum[i]);
}
}
}
```

Program Output

```
Enter 3 X 3 Matrix
45
34
22
67
59
41
20
11
76
Given Matrix is
45 34 22
67 59 41
20 11 76
Column Sum
132 104 139
```

❧❧❧

118] Calculate and print sum of row and column of matrix.

```java
import java.util.*;
public class Program118
{
public static void main()
{
int i,j,rowsum,colsum[] = new int[5];
int mat[][] = new int[5][5];
Scanner scnObj = new Scanner(System.in);
System.out.println("Enter 3 X 3 Matrix");
for(i=0;i<3;i++)
{
for(j=0;j<3;j++)
{
```

```
mat[i][j] = scnObj.nextInt();
}
}
System.out.println("Given Matrix is\t\t\tRow Sum");
for(i=0;i<3;i++)
{
rowsum = 0;
colsum[i] = 0;
for(j=0;j<3;j++)
{
System.out.print("\t"+mat[i][j]);
rowsum +=mat[i][j];
colsum[i] +=mat[j][i];
}
System.out.print("\t"+rowsum);
System.out.println();
}
System.out.println("Column Sum");
for(i=0;i<3;i++)
{
System.out.print("\t"+colsum[i]);
}
}
}
```

Program Output

```
Enter 3 X 3 Matrix
5
4
6
8
7
9
2
```

```
1
3
Given Matrix is Row Sum
5 4 6 15
8 7 9 24
2 1 3 6
Column Sum
15 12 18
```

119] Find maximum number from row of matrix.

```java
import java.util.*;
public class Program119
{
public static void main()
{
int i,j,k,r,c,max;
int mat[][] = new int[5][5];
Scanner scnObj = new Scanner(System.in);
System.out.println("Enter no of rows:");
r = scnObj.nextInt();
System.out.println("Enter no of columns:");
c = scnObj.nextInt();
System.out.println("Enter "+r+"x"+c+" Matrix");
for(i=0;i<r;i++)
{
for(j=0;j<c;j++)
{
mat[i][j] = scnObj.nextInt();
}
}
System.out.println("Given Matrix is :-");
for(i=0;i<r;i++)
```

```
{
for(j=0;j<c;j++)
{
System.out.print("\t"+mat[i][j]);
}
System.out.println();
}
System.out.println("Matrix      -\t\tRow      Maximum
Number.");
for(i=0;i<r;i++)
{
max=mat[i][0];
for(j=0;j<c;j++)
{
if(mat[i][j]>max)
max=mat[i][j];
System.out.print("\t"+mat[i][j]);
}
System.out.print("\t"+max);
System.out.println();
}
}
}
```

Program Output

Enter no of rows:

3

Enter no of columns:

3

Enter 3x3 Matrix

17

58

56

32

```
98
67
33
48
72
Given Matrix is :-
17 58 56
32 98 67
33 48 72
Matrix - Row Maximum Number.
17 58 56 58
32 98 67 98
33 48 72 72
```

***

120] Find maximum number from column of matrix.

```java
import java.util.*;
public class Program120
{
public static void main()
{
int i,j,k,r,c,max, colmax[] = new int[5];
int mat[][] = new int[5][5];
Scanner scnObj = new Scanner(System.in);
System.out.println("Enter no of rows:");
r = scnObj.nextInt();
System.out.println("Enter no of columns:");
c = scnObj.nextInt();
System.out.println("Enter "+r+"x"+c+" Matrix");
for(i=0;i<r;i++)
{
for(j=0;j<c;j++)
{
```

```java
mat[i][j] = scnObj.nextInt();
}
}
System.out.println("Given Matrix is :-");
for(i=0;i<r;i++)
{
for(j=0;j<c;j++)
{
System.out.print("\t"+mat[i][j]);
}
System.out.println();
}
System.out.println("Matrix is");
for(i=0;i<r;i++)
{
colmax[i]=mat[0][i];
for(j=0;j<c;j++)
{
if(mat[j][i]>colmax[i])
colmax[i]=mat[j][i];
System.out.print("\t"+mat[i][j]);
}
System.out.println();
}
System.out.println("Column Maximum number is");
for(i=0;i<c;i++)
{
System.out.print("\t"+colmax[i]);
}
}
}
```

Program Output

Enter no of rows:

3
Enter no of columns:
3
Enter 3x3 Matrix
1
2
3
7
8
9
6
5
4
Given Matrix is :-
1 2 3
7 8 9
6 5 4
Matrix is
1 2 3
7 8 9
6 5 4
Column Maximum number is
7 8 9

121] Find minimum number from row of matrix.

```java
import java.util.*;
public class Program121
{
public static void main()
{
int i,j,k,r,c,min;
int mat[][] = new int[5][5];
```

```java
Scanner scnObj = new Scanner(System.in);
System.out.println("Enter no of rows:");
r = scnObj.nextInt();
System.out.println("Enter no of columns:");
c = scnObj.nextInt();
System.out.println("Enter "+r+"x"+c+" Matrix");
for(i=0;i<r;i++)
{
for(j=0;j<c;j++)
{
mat[i][j] = scnObj.nextInt();
}
}
System.out.println("Given Matrix is :-");
for(i=0;i<r;i++)
{
for(j=0;j<c;j++)
{
System.out.print("\t"+mat[i][j]);
}
System.out.println();
}
System.out.println("Matrix        -\t\tRow        Minimum
Number.");
for(i=0;i<r;i++)
{
min=mat[i][0];
for(j=0;j<c;j++)
{
if(mat[i][j]<min)
min=mat[i][j];
System.out.print("\t"+mat[i][j]);
}
```

```
System.out.print("\t"+min);
System.out.println();
}
}
}
```

Program Output Enter no of rows: 3 Enter no of columns: 3 Enter 3x3 Matrix 1 2 3 7 8 9 6 5 4 Given Matrix is :- 1 2 3 7 8 9 6 5 4 Matrix is 1 2 3 7 8 9 6 5 4 Column Maximum number is 7 8 9

Program Output

Enter no of rows:

3

Enter no of columns:

3

Enter 3x3 Matrix

66

12

43

55

89

10

93

71

37

Given Matrix is :-

66 12 43

55 89 10

93 71 37

Matrix - Row Mininum Number.

66 12 43 12

55 89 10 10

93 71 37 37

122] Find minimum number from column of matrix.

```java
import java.util.*;
public class Program122
{
public static void main()
{
int i,j,k,r,c,max, colmin[] = new int[5];
int mat[][] = new int[5][5];
Scanner scnObj = new Scanner(System.in);
System.out.println("Enter no of rows:");
r = scnObj.nextInt();
System.out.println("Enter no of columns:");
c = scnObj.nextInt();
System.out.println("Enter "+r+"x"+c+" Matrix");
for(i=0;i<r;i++)
{
for(j=0;j<c;j++)
{
mat[i][j] = scnObj.nextInt();
}
}
System.out.println("Given Matrix is :-");
for(i=0;i<r;i++)
{
for(j=0;j<c;j++)
{
System.out.print("\t"+mat[i][j]);
}
System.out.println();
}
System.out.println("Matrix is");
for(i=0;i<r;i++)
```

```
{
colmin[i]=mat[0][i];
for(j=0;j<c;j++)
{
if(mat[j][i]<colmin[i])
colmin[i]=mat[j][i];
System.out.print("\t"+mat[i][j]);
}
System.out.println();
}
System.out.println("Column Minimum number is");
for(i=0;i<c;i++)
{
System.out.print("\t"+colmin[i]);
}
}
}
```

Program Output

Enter no of rows:

3

Enter no of columns:

3

Enter 3x3 Matrix

65

87

12

43

90

23

56

21

33

Given Matrix is :-

65 87 12
43 90 23
56 21 33
Matrix is
65 87 12
43 90 23
56 21 33
Column Minimum number is
43 21 12

CHAPTER ELEVEN

String Programs

123] Calculate string length using strlen() function.

```
public class Program123
{
public static void main(String str)
{
int length;
length = str.length();
System.out.println("Entered string is :- "+str);
System.out.println("Length of string is :- "+length);
}
}
```

Program Output

Entered string is :- Welcome

Length of string is :- 7

124] Calculate string length without using strlen() function.

```
import java.util.*;
public class Program124
{
public static void main()
{
```

```
String name;
int strlength=0;
Scanner scnObj = new Scanner(System.in);
System.out.println("Enter name");
name = scnObj.nextLine();
char[] stringChars = name.toCharArray();
for(char s: stringChars)
strlength++;
System.out.println("Length of String = " +strlength);
}
}
```

Program Output
```
Enter name
Aadishree
Length of String = 9
```

125] Compare Two Strings using compareTo Function.

```
import java.util.*;
public class Program125
{
public static void main()
{
String str1,str2;
int strlength=0;
Scanner scnObj = new Scanner(System.in);
System.out.println("Enter first string");
str1 = scnObj.nextLine();
System.out.println("Enter second string");
str2 = scnObj.nextLine();
if(str1.compareTo(str2)==0)
{
System.out.println("Strings are equal.");
```

```java
}
else
{
System.out.println("Strings are not equal.");
}
}
}
```

Program Output

Enter first string
book
Enter second string
book
Strings are equal.

❦❦❦

126] Compare Two Strings without using equals.

```java
import java.util.*;
public class Program126
{
public static void main()
{
String str1,str2;
int strlength=0;
Scanner scnObj = new Scanner(System.in);
System.out.println("Enter first string");
str1 = scnObj.nextLine();
System.out.println("Enter second string");
str2 = scnObj.nextLine();
if(str1.equals(str2)==true)
{
System.out.println("Strings are equal.");
}
else
```

```
{
System.out.println("Strings are not equal.");
}
}
}
```

Program Output

Enter first string

Pen

Enter second string

Pen

Strings are equal.

❧❧❧

127] Copy string using strcpy() function.

```
import java.util.*;
public class Program127
{
public static void main()
{
String destStr,sourceStr;
Scanner scnObj = new Scanner(System.in);
System.out.println("Enter source string");
sourceStr = scnObj.nextLine();
destStr = String.valueOf(sourceStr);
System.out.println("Source String :- "+sourceStr);
System.out.println("Destination String :- "+destStr);
}
}
```

Program Output

Enter source string

welcome

Source String :- welcome

Destination String :- welcome

128] Concanate two strings using strcat() function.

```
import java.util.*;
public class Program128
{
public static void main()
{
String str;
Scanner scnObj = new Scanner(System.in);
System.out.println("Enter string");
str = scnObj.nextLine();
System.out.println("4th character "+str.charAt(3));
}
}
```

Program Output

```
Enter string
Today
4th character a
```

129] Concanate two strings without using strcat() function.

```
public class Program129
{
public static void main()
{
String str;
str = "Success";
System.out.println("String is "+str);
System.out.println("Index of e is "+ str.indexOf('e'));
}
}
```

Program Output
String is Success
Index of e is 4

130] Replace character in a string.

```
public class Program130
{
public static void main()
{
String str,newStr;
str = "happy home";
System.out.println("String is :- "+str);
newStr = str.replace('h','H');
System.out.println("New string is :- "+newStr);
}
}
```

Program Output
String is :- happy home
New string is :- Happy Home

131] Convert string into upper case.

```
import java.util.*;
public class Program131
{
public static void main()
{
String str,newStr;
Scanner scnObj = new Scanner(System.in);
System.out.println("Enter string in lowercase");
str = scnObj.nextLine();
newStr = str.toUpperCase();
```

```
System.out.println("String in Upper Case:- "+newStr);
}
}
```

Program Output

Enter string in lowercase

happy home

String in Upper Case:- HAPPY HOME

❧❧❧

132] Convert string into lower case.

```
import java.util.*;
public class Program132
{
public static void main()
{
String str,newStr;
Scanner scnObj = new Scanner(System.in);
System.out.println("Enter string in uppercase");
str = scnObj.nextLine();
newStr = str.toLowerCase();
System.out.println("String in Lower Case:- "+newStr);
}
}
```

Program Output

Enter string in uppercase

HAPPY HOME

String in Lower Case:- happy home

❧❧❧

CHAPTER TWELVE

Function Programs

133] Addition of two nos. using function.

```java
import java.util.*;
public class Program133
{
public static void main()
{
int p,q,a,b,sum;
Scanner scnObj = new Scanner(System.in);
System.out.println("Enter first no.");
p = scnObj.nextInt();
System.out.println("Enter second no.");
q = scnObj.nextInt();
sum = addition(p,q);
System.out.println("Addition of two numbers :- "+sum);
}
static int addition(int a, int b)
{
return a+b;
}
}
```

Program Output
Enter first no.
34

```
Enter second no.
67
Addition of two numbers :- 101
```

134] Calculate area of circle using function.

```java
import java.util.*;
public class Program134
{
public static void main()
{
double pi=3.14, r;
double ac;
Scanner scnObj = new Scanner(System.in);
System.out.println("Enter Radius of Circle.");
r = scnObj.nextDouble();
ac = areacircle(r,pi);
System.out.println("Area of circle is "+ac);
}
static double areacircle(double r,double pi)
{
return pi * r * r;
}
}
```

Program Output

```
Enter Radius of Circle.
5
Area of circle is 78.5
```

❧❧❧

135] Calculate area of square using function.

```java
import java.util.*;
public class Program135
{
public static void main()
```

```
{
int side,area;
Scanner scnObj = new Scanner(System.in);
System.out.println("Enter side.");
side = scnObj.nextInt();
area = areaofsquare(side);
System.out.println("Area of square :- "+area);
}
static int areaofsquare(int side)
{
return side * side;
}
}
```

Program Output
```
Enter side.
4
Area of square :- 16
```

136] Calculate area of rectangle using function.
```
import java.util.*;
public class Program136
{
public static void main()
{
int a,l,b;
Scanner scnObj = new Scanner(System.in);
System.out.println("Enter length.");
l= scnObj.nextInt();
System.out.println("Enter breadth.");
b = scnObj.nextInt();
a = area(l,b);
System.out.println("Area of rectangle :- "+a);
```

```
}
static int area(int l, int b)
{
return l*b;
}
}
```

Program Output

Enter length.

6

Enter breadth.

7

Area of rectangle :- 42